GW01239692

ZEN AND THE ART OF
[nothing]

METAPHYSICS IN POETRY

A SYSTEM TO SEE BUSINESS, LIFE, AND REALITY BETTER

JOHN ZDANOWSKI & JEFF ABRAMS

Published by CoAuthor.one

For our children

Caroline, Jack, Celia, Luke, Mila, Levi & Jake

their children

so on.

To *soften* your relationship with the stories you've heard,

To *strengthen* your relationship with the stories you tell.

CONTENTS

ZEN AND THE ART OF [nothing]

∞

CHAPTER 1

What is Good?

Whatw is your philosophy? I've asked this question of many people for many years. Though few can articulate it clearly, everyone has a philosophy. I was handed a philosophy that I was expected to accept without question. For a long time, I did accept it without question.

DEFINITION OF A GOOD LIFE

A philosophy is how we define and decide "What is Good?" Philosophers ask questions like "What is a Good Life?" and "How does one live a Good Life?"

The philosophy that had been handed down to me was the traditional definition of 20th-century success in the United States:

- Get good grades to get into a good college,
- Have a paper route to save money for college,
- Become an Eagle Scout to win a scholarship to pay for college,
- Study things in college to get a good job,

- Work 50 or 60 hours a week until you retire,
- Mow your grass, rake your leaves, save for retirement,
- Go to church every Sunday, thy will be done.

The paper route was the most dangerous time of my day. Every morning, from 12 to 18 years old, I got up at 6 am and delivered newspapers to 50 to 100 homes in my neighborhood. Ever week, I'd get on my bicycle and collect hundreds of dollars of cash. They don't even let kids have this job anymore. But that's not why it was dangerous. It was dangerous because it gave me quiet time to think and watch glimpses of people lives. In my neighborhood, we all seemed to have been given similar philosophies. It felt like we were *programmed* to be this way. Geography is destiny, I thought.

Within one square mile of where I was born, I saw a narrow range of lifestyles. I saw very normal people, with very normal jobs, doing very normal things like raking leaves. For some reason, as a teenager, I couldn't imagine anything worse.

At 14 years old, I started to add things to my list of what it meant to have a Good Life:

~ Not having to rake your own leaves. ~

I decided then that I would live a life where I would not have to rake my own leaves. In the meantime, I accepted the programming I was given, and I did what I was told. I got up every morning and delivered newspapers. I cut people's lawns and raked their leaves. I did my homework, got straight A's, and got scholarships to help pay for college. I graduated college in three years and started at General Electric in one of their "prestigious" engineering and management training programs.

I was rewarded with a cubicle in a windowless lab and...

~ *I hated it from day one.* ~

Whoops. This was *not good*, I thought. Now what?

[nothing] is an exploration of *how we aim to live*. It celebrates the fiftieth anniversary of Robert Pirsig's classic *Zen and the Art of Motorcycle Maintenance: An Inquiry into Values*. That book opened with this epigraph:

> *"And what is good, Phaedrus, and what is not good—Need we ask anyone to tell us these things?"*

I remembered a set of signs I put on the wall of my college dormitory, Birth, School, Work, Death, and this poem appeared.

~ BIRTH, SCHOOL, WORK, DEATH ~

A poem about the pointlessness of life in the machine

Input, process, output.
Food, the use, and waste
Feeds another system,
That must
Consume
In haste.

Delays just make us hungry
And burn what was desire
To try to make a difference
Or just
toss it in
the fire.

Input, process, output.
The Word, your brain, your job.
Feeding you some money,
Your life,
It seems,
They rob.

In truth, you are the giver,
Of time to the machine,
Retirement the vision
Of some
Future life
Serene.

CHAPTER 2

What We Are Supposed To Do

I landed in a job that I hated because I was *supposed* to land there. I was an electrical engineer working in a windowless lab in what felt like the most sunless city in America.

One February, the news said there was only 20 hours of sunshine for the entire month. I had to take their word for it because I am certain I didn't see it. People need the sun, I thought.

My brother fell into the same spot seven years before and it seemed to be working for him. It wasn't going to work for me. I could not do this 5 day per week, 50 weeks per year, for 40 years until I retired. This was *Not Good*. I had to *get out*.

Still, I got up and went to work the next day and the next. It was what *I was supposed to do. Chop Wood, Carry*

Water[1], I thought.

Being the Good Student that I was, I read a lot of books to figure out what went wrong.

I read self-help books, business books, and philosophy books. *Brave New World, 1984, What Color is Your Parachute? Think and Grow Rich, Do You Want to be a Lawyer? Seven Habits of Highly Effective People, Aristotle for Everybody, Sophie's World*, and so on.

It was then, in 1991 that I first read *Zen and the Art of Motorcycle Maintenance: An Inquiry into Values* by Robert Pirsig and his second book, *Lila: An Inquiry into Morals*. I filled them both with highlights, scribbles, and notes.

> *"The test of the machine is the satisfaction it gives you," Pirsig wrote. "There isn't any other test. If the machine produces tranquility, it's right. If it disturbs you, it's wrong until either the machine or your mind is changed."*

Pure brilliance, I thought.

---

[1] "Chop wood, carry water" is a reference to a Zen koan, a paradoxical statement or question used in Zen practice to provoke deep thought and meditation. This saying encapsulates the idea that enlightenment does not necessarily change the external actions of a person but transforms their inner understanding and experience of those actions.

IF YOU'RE NOT HAPPY, GET HAPPY

At the time, I was living with my friend Pete Radosta in the top half of a 50-year-old house in a city neighborhood with big houses and wide streets.

Pete or "Speedo" as we called him, was my Resident Advisor and next-door neighbor. Among his many accomplishments, he became a Resident Director, founded the Sigma Chi Fraternity and was recognized with our school's highest honor - the Phalanx Leadership Award.

Speedo graduated a year before me, moved to Syracuse, and took a job at a well-respected engineering firm.

~ And his mom and dad thought it was Good. ~

One day, Speedo came home and said he was going to quit his job and move to Park City, Utah. Confusion flooded my mind. This was 1991. Working remotely was not an option. The Internet existed, but the language of hypertext and web browsers had not yet been invented. Most people had landlines. No one had cell phones.

"What are you going to do for work?" I asked.

"Ski Patrol," Speedo said.

Ski Patrol?! With two words, he broke all the rules I'd been taught about life. "You're not allowed to do that," I

14

thought. "You studied civil engineering, and you have a Good Job at a Good engineering firm. *That is what you are supposed to do!*"

As we packed up his U-Haul, I peppered him with questions. "What are you thinking? What about your career? What do your parents think?"

Speedo put his finger up in the air, pausing my torrent of questions. The wind stopped, and the street got quiet. He put his hand on my shoulder and looked me in the eye and said,

"If you're not happy, get happy."

I was stunned. In the silence, Pirsig's words echoed in my mind, "There isn't any other test."

As Speedo drove west, I contemplated the path of my life. As the youngest of four children – I had followed in the footsteps of my older brothers:

We all got paper routes, part-time jobs at restaurants, and went to college to get *Good Jobs*. It seemed *Good* for them. But for me, it was *Not Good.*

It was time to ask more questions.

I began questioning everything from the religion of my parents to the idea of retirement as a worthy goal.

~ IF I COULD ASK ANY QUESTION ~

If I could ask any question,
Where would I start?
Would I ask about music?
Would I ask about art?

Would I ask about conquest?
And power and pain?
Or ask about truth
And justice or rain?

Would I ask about God?
Or ask about men?
Commandments or laws
And what about Zen?

Would I ask what to value?
Would I ask what to do?
Why am I here?
And what about you?

What thing, if you knew it,
Would make your life better?
Ask it and ask it,
But don't wait for a letter.

All human knowledge of
What seems to be known
Won't help you right now
So put down your phone.

Insights don't come
From scrolling at night.
Just sit quietly, dear,
And tap into what's right.

CHAPTER 3

Existential Questions

After asking a lot of questions, I concluded that getting an MBA would be a more socially acceptable way to jump out of this airplane that was going somewhere I didn't want to go. My brother had completed his MBA while working at GE, but I was finally going to be different and go full time.

While I was completing applications to a variety of business schools, my dad asked,

~ *"Are you going to apply to Harvard?"* ~

"No, Dad," I snapped as if my dad had no way to know what he was talking about.

There was no way he could know what he was talking about. My dad spent one year at Saint John Fisher College before dropping out and becoming a sheet metal worker - a Good Union Job.

"Your name isn't on any buildings," I continued, completely rejecting his idea. "We don't even know anyone who has ever visited there! There's no way I'll get in! It would be a waste of time and money to apply."

My Dad was used to my overconfident certitude. He thought about it for a minute, then, a wry smile slowly lit up his face. "Ok, John, I'll bet you $100 that you'll get in."

We grew up playing cards and gambling for money with family almost every week. Calculating odds was one of the highest-valued skills a person could have in a family, in life, and, by extension, in the world.

This bet didn't require calculation. I had already written dozens of essays applying to other schools. A few more essays would be easy enough to slap together and win this bet.

"Ok, Dad, you're on."

One of the essay questions was:

WHAT WOULD I DO WITH A HARVARD MBA

For the first time in my life, *I had no brothers to follow.* It was time to write my own story. I wrote:

After graduating from Harvard Business School, I plan to work at a management consulting firm. I'd like to gain experience with a variety of companies rapidly. I believe that will provide a capstone of practical business experience after business school in the same way that the rotational program at GE did after college.

After that, I would like to experience buying and selling companies.

Then, I would get experience with starting and growing companies before starting a company on my own.

Ultimately, I plan to start and run my own company. I believe the experience and network I would gain by attending Harvard Business School, followed by the right set of experiences, would dramatically increase my likelihood of success.

After building my company, I would write a book and teach.

I lost the bet and moved to Boston. And Boston had the best weather I'd ever lived in.

Looking back on it, years later, I realized everything I wrote about my aspirations for my life happened...in order.

How is that possible?

The only aspiration that I had written in that essay that hadn't yet happened was...that I would write a book.

~ So, I started writing. ~

~ PRACTICAL PHILOSOPHICAL TRUTH ~

~ *Practical* ~

An Unintentional Haiku by my father.

You're never gonna
Make any real money just
Work'n for someone else.

~ *Philosophical* ~

Inspired by a descendant of the last Chief of the Comanche

I am the father of my sons
I am the one who comes before
I am the son of many men
Who struggled in life and war.

~ *Truth* ~

The "Boot Sequence" as explained by a friend

Today is the best day ever.
I am free to do whatever I want
I am the master of my universe and
I am the narrator of my own epic story.

CHAPTER 4

How Do We Know What We Know?

In the first chapter of Robert Pirsig's second book, *Lila - An Inquiry into Morals,* he described his system for writing. He had "four long card-catalog-type trays" containing eleven thousand cards that he spent "four years organizing and reorganizing."

I remember writing in the margins:

~ *A system to pursue Quality.* ~

My process was similar, if a bit more electronic and less meticulously organized. Wherever I was I wrote - mostly with no purpose or agenda. I imagined I was filling an appendix.

One of the memos I wrote in the appendix was, "People are like Sonar Systems."

~

PEOPLE ARE LIKE SONAR SYSTEMS

On a family vacation in England visiting cousins, I walked around the Chithurst Monastery a couple hours southwest of London. I thought about the role of rigid routines, practices, and beliefs and how different people throughout the world all viewed the world differently.

In the silence and solitude of the monastery grounds, I wondered, how do people know what to believe? I wondered how people separate the signal from the noise?

As an electrical engineer in that windowless office, I worked on a sonar system. A sonar does three things, it:

- Samples data from its environment,
- Separates the signal from the noise, and
- Creates a map of the territory.

People seem to do the same thing sonar systems do. They:

- Gather data from their senses and stories they are told,
- Separate the data they value from data they don't value,
- Create a mental map from what they value to determine what to pursue and how they should behave.

~ SIGNAL AND NOISE ~

What is the signal, and what is the noise?
What is reality, and what is the ploy?
What is the sickness, and what is the well?
What part is heaven, and what part is hell?

What can you know before being taught?
What can you see before there is thought?
What is the moon, and what is the sun?
What hasn't started, and what has begun?

What is so pure, and what is diluted?
Who has the truth, and who is deluded?
What is the root, and what is the tree?
Can we be separate or one you and me?

Is there a path? Is there a way?
To shuffle the clutter from here to away?
Why is there earth, and why is there air?
Everything wiped out with one solar flare.

What is religion, and what is the way?
Why should we listen t'what you have to say?
What is the seed, and what is the flower?
How would it be different if you had the power?

What is the tree, and what is the leaf?
To what do you point at as your source of belief?
What is the food, and what is the waste?
Would it still all exist if we had to be chaste?

Before you were born, long after you're dead,
What will they mean - these thoughts in your head?

CHAPTER 5

These Thoughts in Your Head

I grew up in Rochester, New York. My parents have been married for 64 years. They have 4 kids, 12 grandchildren, and 8 great-grandchildren. They and all their spouses live in or within driving distance of Rochester. I love my family, so, I live in San Diego.

~

One weekend, two of my seven nephews, Jeff Abrams and Phil Zdanowski, came to visit. Jeff is twenty years younger than me, and Phil is a bit younger than Jeff.

Jeff and I began working together when he graduated college. I was his mentor, now he is mine. We formed a business together in 2021 as equal partners. Sometimes, it's difficult for a mentor-mentee relationship to evolve into something new. As we were forming the partnership, Jeff said, "Do you know how valuable I am?"

I replied, "Do you want more than 50%?"

[nothing] is derived from the conversations we've had almost every day since. It is the philosophy of our

partnership. The philosophy of how we aspire to operate in the world. We expect the system will evolve.

∞

Phil was our first employee. He had been working at a CPA firm for four years. It was sucking the life out of him. He worked for ungrateful clients who viewed audits as an expensive, useless, necessary evil.

Phil thought he would work hard and get promoted to manager in ten years, then it would be *Good*. I told him, "That's a terrible story, Phil. Stop telling yourself that story."

~ *I'd rather rake other people's leaves.* ~

Sipping iced tea and contemplating business and life with my nephews I leaned toward Phil, looked him in the eye, and said, "I used to think my thoughts were true."

Phil was stunned. "You have to believe your thoughts are true! Don't you? What are your thoughts to you?"

We laughed at the Dr. Suess-like cadence of that interchange. I can't think of anything better than sitting with my nephews for a weekend, sipping iced tea.

~ THE THINKER & THE NAUGHT ~

A poem about consciousness and the contents of consciousness.[2]

I used to think my thoughts were true.

> *You have to believe your thoughts are true*
> *Without your thoughts, who are you?*

I used to think my thoughts were me.

> *If they aren't you… Then who are thee?*
> *I am the thinker let me be!*
> *I control that string of thoughts.*
> *I am the thinker, am I not?*

Just sit and think a string of thought.
Are you the thinker or the naught?

I used to think that I decided.
Which thoughts got through and which got sided.

But that was just another thought
That bubbled up above the naught.

---

[2] Inspired by Byron Katie's *Loving What Is*
https://thework.com/instruction-the-work-byron-katie/ and
Sam Harris's *Waking up: A Guide to Spirituality Without Religion*
https://www.wakingup.com/

CHAPTER 6

A Map of Things Inside Your Head

D espite 12 years of religious indoctrination as a child, I didn't learn to meditate until I turned 50.

~ How come that's not a sin? ~

They teach us all this stuff, but they don't teach us how our minds work. It is as if science doesn't really know.

In guided meditations, we are asked to notice various things that arise in consciousness and then fall away. Sam Harris calls these things the "Contents of Consciousness."

Consciousness is the unchanging "naught" in which everything we experience appears. Whether the inputs creating the contents of consciousness come from our day-to-day activity in the world, or from a computer simulation built by the overlords in The Matrix, consciousness is the space where our experience of life appears.

~ *Venn Diagram: Consciousness and its Contents* ~

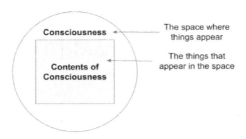

Meditation teachers prompt us, first, to notice our breath, then the sounds around us, then the thoughts in our heads. One of the things they teach you at Harvard Business School is how to think in 2x2s – so this picture appeared in my head.

THE 2X2 OF THE CONTENTS OF CONSCIOUSNESS

	No Words	Words
Internal	Breath	Thought
External	Breeze	Stories

Everything that passes through consciousness falls into one of the 2x2 blocks. Consider how *Breath* and *Thought* are similar.

We can make ourselves breathe rapidly or slowly; at the same time, we can just ignore it, and breathing still happens.

Thought is the same way. We can focus our attention on a subject and maybe, write a sentence. Yet at the same time, thoughts still form endlessly without any effort.

Bringing it outside the body, Breeze represents all the wordless things in our environments that we feel and affect us. We have no control over them.

The line down the middle of the 2x2 is important. On the left of the line is life before words and on the right is life after words. It's such an important line that it's one of the most famous lines in The Bible - *"In the beginning, was the word."*

~ *Why?* ~

It's easy to forget the awesome power of The Word that each of us thoughtlessly wields. Before words, nature's ability to transmit information through generations was severely limited. When we acquired the ability to use words everything changed - a new beginning for the planet, and for humanity.

It's like we ate from some kind of tree of knowledge.

~ SUBTLE CHOICE ~

A poem about choice in the Garden of Eden

Assume Garden of Eden
How would you behave?
Would you be the foolish one?
Or would you be the knave?

Would you fight for all our innocence?
Or fight for knowledge true
To speak The Word like gods
Or bathe in morning dew.

Who will decide for all?
The One! Yes! The Decider
Would she say what's right and wrong?
And who would sit beside her?

I'd rather let each one decide
A much more subtle choice
To succumb to death and homicide
Or learn to use your voice.

CHAPTER 7

The Word is not The Thing

As the lack of sun sucked the life out of me in that windowless lab, I did appreciate GE's Edison Engineering Program. The program was named after Thomas Edison, the founder of GE. I thanked God for the inventor of the light bulb, those were some dark days.

Edison did something that few people in the history of humanity have ever done. Imagine founding a company and having it last over 100 years. Edison said,

"If we all did the things
we are really capable of doing,
we would literally astound ourselves."

For part of the Edison program, we had to solve a variety of complicated word problems related to the technologies underlying Radar and Sonar Systems. We wrote long-hand reports with sentences explaining the complicated math.

WORDS AND MATH MAKE SCIENCE

Mathematics is a highly precise form of language. When words and math combine to predict things, we call that science.

Different communities of people use different words more frequently than other communities - even within the same language. For example, one word that I never heard before living in San Diego is "moment" as in "being in the..."

After learning to meditate, I was talking to a Lyft driver and naturally, the subject of "being in the moment" came up. He said, "Have you read this book?" He reached into his passenger seat and held "*The Wisdom of Insecurity*," by Alan Watts.

~ *When the student is ready, the teacher will appear* ~

I ordered the book immediately. It was my first introduction to Alan Watts. Born in England, Alan Watts spent the 1960's living on a houseboat in Sausalito. I imagined there were no leaves to rake on a houseboat.

Watts is credited for being one of the first people to make Eastern philosophies accessible to Western audiences. Watts had a unique ability to blend profound insights with a conversational style, making complex ideas about mindfulness, existence, and the nature of reality understandable.

Since then, I've read and listened to his prolific works. One of his more famous speeches was set to music and turned into a song. It starts:

> *"I wonder, I wonder, what you would do...if*
> *you had the power to dream any dream you*
> *wanted to."*[3]

Watts's pointed me to another 20th century philosopher named Alfred Korzybski. Born in Poland in the late 1800s, Korzybski followed his father's instructions to become an engineer as well. He emigrated to the US around the turn of the century and developed a branch of philosophy called General Semantics.

General Semantics is the study of how language and symbols influence human thought and behavior. It aims to improve communication and critical thinking by making people more aware of the assumptions and interpretations that underlie their use of language.

---

[3] See https://weeklyaccounting.com/inspiration/

Korzybski coined the phrase "the map is not the territory" and "the word is not the thing." These lines highlight how language can point at, but never fully express, the full spectrum of reality.

In 1937, Korzybski gave a seminar series on General Semantics at Olivet College. As I read it, I could feel myself sitting in the audience. It starts:

~ *"To begin with, lose all fear."* ~

As I was summarizing my understanding of it, this *Not-a-Poem* appeared.

~ Using Language Like Math ~

A poem about how language affects our perceptions

Everything is either that or not that.
Things that are kind of like that
Are not that.
Anything that can be pointed at or thought of
Is either that or not that.

See for yourself.
It's a test of sorts.
An inarguable truth.

Sometimes, you can find things that break the rule.
Even a rule as simple as that.

You might find, for example, a mammal that lays eggs.
Mammals don't lay eggs,
That's the definition of a mammal,
And yet, a mammal that lays eggs
Is called a platypus.

If you find too many platypuses,
In your math or in your language,
Then it's time to question
Your first principles, your generalizations,
The implicit assumptions embedded in your language.

*Inevitably, when you face a situation frankly, a solution
appears. This has been true for the whole history of
civilization.*[4]

Insight never appears before it does.

---

[4] Alfred Korzybski, *General Semantics Seminar 1937: Olivet College
Lectures*

CHAPTER 8

The Art of Complicated Subjects

Wow. You've come a long way. Let's rest here and see how far we've come.

We've covered:

- How a philosophy defines *What is Good,*
- That philosophies are *lessons passed through generations,*
- How everything we do in our lives seems to start as a *story in our heads,*
- How *we* separate the signal from the noise and make a *map of the territory* to *know what we know,*
- The difference between *consciousness* and the *contents of consciousness,* and
- That the *words we use* and the stories we tell *affect how we perceive* the world.

We have braved some significant philosophical territory and we're still hiking up the mountain. This is "the high country of the mind" as Pirsig called it. He said,

"Mountains should be climbed with as little effort as possible and without desire. The reality of your own nature should determine the speed. If you become restless, speed up. If you become winded, slow down. You climb the

*mountain in an equilibrium between
restlessness and exhaustion."*

Zen and the Art of Motorcycle Maintenance was filled with insights like this. On the surface, it's a simple story. Robert Pirsig and his son are on a motorcycle trip from Minneapolis through the Dakotas, Montana, and into the Pacific Northwest. We follow them on their journey and learn about the different ways to care for a motorcycle on a long trip.

There's a second storyline in the book that is a lot more complicated. During the long motorcycle rides from place to place, Pirsig narrates the story of how his younger self, who he has named Phaedrus, was committed to an insane asylum for seeing the world differently.

Pirsig calls his way of seeing the world the Metaphysics of Quality. Metaphysics is a way of slicing up the world so we can better understand it. Think of it as a "map" of reality. Pirsig said,

*"We take a handful of sand from the endless
landscape of awareness around us and call that
handful of sand the world."*

A Metaphysics is a Map of Reality

Aristotle called metaphysics the first philosophy. A metaphysics slices up the world so we can better understand explain and predict it. Aristotle's first slice of reality was between subjects and objects. According to that slice, each of us are *subjects* in the world that experience the *objects* in the world. Aristotle's metaphysics is the one we all commonly understand. The entirety of *western science and thought* is based on this first slice.

~ *Pirsig sliced the world differently* ~

Instead of fixed subjects and objects, Pirsig describes a world in constant flux all trending ineffably toward Quality. He described four levels of change, each building on the other, with different characteristics and timescales of change.

At the base level of Pirsig's Quality is Inorganic Quality – the Earth, as an example. Just above that is Organic Quality, as in life on Earth. Just above that is Cultural Quality, as in the way living organisms organize themselves. And finally, at the top is Intellectual Quality which comprises all the ideas and patterns of thought that we have about the world.

Quality

	Static Patterns	Dynamic Patterns
Intellectual Science, Philosophy, Spirituality	Traditional Schools of Thought	New Ideas Discoveries Misinformation
Cultural Psychology & Economics	Countries Companies Organizations	War Elections Markets Competition
Organic Biology & Evolution	Life	Biological Evolution Mutations Viruses
Inorganic Physics & Chemistry	Matter	Weather Earthquakes

Each of these levels of Quality is split into Static Patterns and Dynamic Patterns. For example, DNA is a Static Pattern of Quality, and a mutation is a Dynamic Pattern of Quality.

In this language, *Science* is a Static Pattern of Intellectual Quality. New ideas - like the Earth being round and not being the center of the universe are initially rejected as crazy for a long time before they are accepted as science. In *Lila*, Pirsig said:

> *"Without Dynamic Quality, the organism cannot grow. Without Static Quality the organism cannot last. Both are needed."*

While considering a world without Quality, Pirsig wrote:

> *"Poetry would disappear, since it seldom makes sense and has no practical value."*

And then this poem appeared.

~ EVOLUTION ~

A poem about the Metaphysics of Quality.

Born in garden sunlight
In harmony with Spring
Living off the landscape
Like every living thing

Rivers smooth the mountains
Animals trim the trees
People help each other
In the evening breeze

Lessons passed through generations
Sharing information slow
Communication speeds up
Ending status quo

Stories group the people
Ideas swarm like bees
People fight each other
For imaginary needs

There is no way to stop it
The Word exacts its price
Defining Us distinct from
Them was our only vice

CHAPTER 9

Meta-What?

Metaphysics is a big word, and that makes it sound like a complicated subject. When big words and complicated subjects come up, you can almost hear people's brains click off.

~ *Click* ~

Complicated subjects have been institutionalized in what Pirsig calls the Church of Reason ~ educational institutions that certify people with degrees to convey their authority on a particular subject. Educational institutions frequently teach

~ *Static Patterns of intellectual Quality.* ~

When a new idea appears, especially one that cuts across disciplines in a new way, it's difficult for institutionalized people to see the new idea. Frequently the people in the institutions see the people who think differently as a threat, and they institutionalize people who think differently to maintain the status quo.

INSTALLING A CULTURAL STORY

People in institutions of higher learning form a kind of priesthood. Many of these priesthoods were formed around beliefs etched in stone generations before people knew the world was round.

Education systems rotely pass on the stories accepted by the priesthoods and politicians to children.

LESSONS PASSED THROUGH GENERATIONS

We memorize dates, events, people, and stories important to our country's founding, history, and development of our constitution and our economy. We learn about the challenges people before us faced and overcame. This is how countries pass on and preserve the stories of their culture.

~ BETWEEN CONTROL AND CHAOS ~

Different cultural systems bubble up and disappear. A few persist. People struggle for resources within their cultural systems and in the clash of cultural systems.

New technologies and new ideas change cultures. Better systems inevitably proliferate or reach a tenuous balance of cultural market share.

Status quo is an illusion. Everything changes.

The Histomap of World History[5]

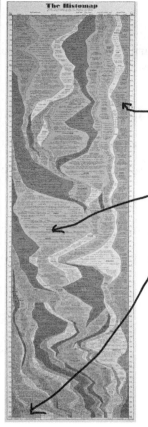

The Histomap is a view of history that shows how different cultural systems bubble up and disappear.

Shrunk to fit this book, three things are notable.

1. China is the only unbroken chain. It stretches from the top right of the poster all the way to the bottom right. No other country has persisted as it has for as long.

2. The big bubble in the middle of the poster is the Roman Empire. No other cultural story has ever dominated the world as much.

3. The United States appears in the last bit of the poster on the lower left. Its barely visible.

From this perspective it's easier to see that society is a ceaseless dance between control and chaos. What Pirsig called "Static Quality" and "Dynamic Quality."

---

[5] The Histomap was designed by John B. Sparks and originally published by Rand McNally in 1931. It's available as a beautiful six-foot-tall poster at TheHistomap.com.

43

It usually takes a *Brujo* - a crazy person – to change things. Sometimes it's just a crazy person's idea driving change.

Consider an idea as simple as wearing helmets when we ski.

FROM CRACKED SKULLS TO CRAZY PEOPLE

When I first learned to ski, nobody wore a helmet. If you saw a person wearing a helmet, you might think they had a cracked skull.

Today, everyone wears a helmet. If you see someone *not* wearing a helmet, you might think they need to have their head examined.

If you plotted the percentage of people not wearing a helmet over time from then until now, it would look like this:

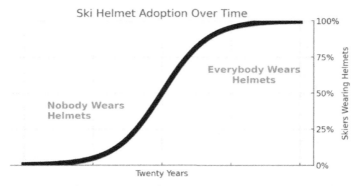

The adoption of new ideas always follows this curve.

44

Initially, nobody wore helmets while skiing. A few famous people broke their skulls on trees, and now nearly everybody wears helmets.

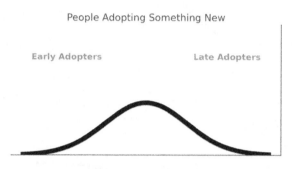

Some people are early adopters, some later.

HOW SYSTEMS EVOLVE

Such change across populations is common. There have been early and late adopters of every new idea and technology.

We see it in the decades of transition from landlines to cell phones.

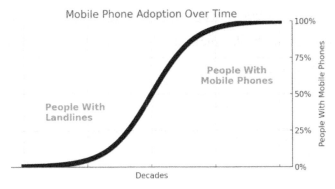

No one has landlines anymore.

We see it in the eon's long transition from early humans to Homo Sapiens.

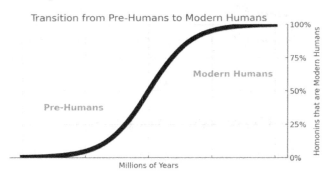

There are no more Neanderthals

It is similar in the adoption of housing, running water, sanitation systems, electricity, color televisions, cable televisions, and the Internet. There was a time before everything in our lives. Something appears and changes everything.

~ Click ~

~ THAT CLICK ~

A poem about what causes change

Did you hear that? **That click.**
A gear long stuck was freed
To spin another story
To rewrite every creed.

Did you hear that? **That whir.**
A fan's long silent slices blur.
Blade cuts through guts and blows the air
The smell of blood is everywhere.

Did you hear that? **That grind.**
That freed gear,
It seems, has spun
Another long stuck over here.

Did you see that? **That flash.**
The blind went up, a crack of light
Streams through pane
To bathe the blight.

Do you feel that? **That breeze.**
Through that broken window
The smoke and pain of war
I'm certain it will never be as it was before.

Did you hear that? **That sigh.**
Dusty faces staring
A mother holding baby
Too stunned to even cry.

CHAPTER 10

How Ideas Proliferate

S ome ideas and some stories are labeled "divinely inspired." We are told that a single founder had some special connection to the divine that you *don't have,* and you *can never* have.

There are stories like this in every culture. Before Jesus, there was no Christianity. Before Mohammad, no Islam.

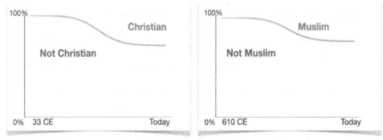

A tenuous balance of cultural market share.

A TENUOUS BALANCE OF CULTURAL MARKET SHARE

Religious systems spread according to the same function – early adopters and late adopters. Religions never reach 100% of the population. They reach a tenuous balance of cultural market share.

These religious stories were documented in holy books centuries ago and can no longer be edited or even questioned.

I wondered *what makes a book a bible?*

~ NOT-A-BIBLE ~

What makes a book a "bible"
The ones that mustn't budge
Is only their longevity
Letting everybody fudge.

Some words are weak, stories confused
Some are just plain weird
Its strength was never clarity
Just old men, most with beard.

It must not change, it is the truth,
Just how…you're left to judge.
Just not for all humanity
See, only for yourself.

But that's not how these books were used
The truth was hard to see
These books were used by men
For wealth and polity

But if a "bible" could evolve
I wonder what it'd say
The choices of what's written
Still left to men this way.

It would be weird with many truths
Arguing this or *thats*
But that's exactly what we have
As a matter of the facts.

We all carry a bible
Our mind, Our map, Our judge
It's there, at least, subconsciously
Our own stories to fudge.   So…

Make any book your bible
Write what you think is true
Write exactly opposite
Then notice, please God, the hew.

CHAPTER 11

The Religion of Startups

L et's back away from religion and move to something I'm a little more qualified to talk about - startups.

~ A STARTUP RELIGION ~

A person sat in square and thought
Some things they'd never know would wrought
The world would change with just a thought
God loves us all, or we'd be naught.

~

Since business school, I've spent the bulk of my career working with founders and startups. When change driven by the Internet rippled through an industry, I was there. I was attracted by big visions and, as the CFO, I fixed the unit economics.

I worked with computer companies, copier companies, phone companies, and toy companies. I helped to build internet service providers, web hosting companies, and data centers. I took two companies public and helped manage the digital economy of the largest virtual world before Bitcoin.

More recently, the team and I have worked with companies driving change in our US education and healthcare systems.

We also invented a way to lend money against the inventory of emerging consumer brands based on their business data from ecommerce-based platforms like Shopify. This business is called Assembled Brands.

From our experience across these companies and industries, we've heard many founders tell some crazy stories.

THE SPECTRUM OF FOUNDER DELUSION

While a few of these founders might express some spiritual connection to their mission and express it with religious zeal, none would claim to have any more special connection with the divine than you or me.

Founders of startups - be they startup companies, startup schools, startup governments, or startup religions - rely on the ones who come before them.

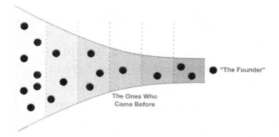

The Ones Who
Came Before

"The Founder"

Founders must invite and recruit others to grow their stories. The early team and investors then, in turn, act like apostles to help the founder tell their stories.

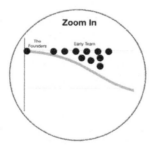

~ A LITTLE SYSTEM ~

There is a little system
to help you with your dream
Say it very clearly
Harder than it might seem

Put the story in the system
Project it with the light
Soon, an image will appear
Almost but not quite right

The system needs some data,
To project reality,
Clear your mind of dreams, my child,
It's time to really see.

It'll take a few more people,
To make our dreams come true,
To help us tell the story, and
Focus on what's true.

It'll get a little better,
Each time you risk to share,
Incorporate the feedback,
Put down your ego bear.

But the system is much simpler,
Than this poem makes it sound,
Just say your dream out loud, my friend,
And then just write it down.

CHAPTER 12

A Big Vision Story

One Saturday, while we were building Assembled Brands, Trevor, the head of growth, came to my house for the day. We spent the entire day and evening in what might be best, classified as an entheogenic strategy and coaching session.

Trevor was a 35-year-old, six-foot-four, fit, brilliant Indian man skilled with technology and growth hacking. He overflowed with confidence and positivity.

At one point during the day, he asked, "What do you tell yourself when you wake up in the morning?"

A flood of messages of grief and anxiety filled my awareness in response to his question.

I laughed uncomfortably and told him, "I usually think things like 'I drank too much last night. I stayed up too late. I devoured the rest of the ice cream. I have a stomachache." Organic anxiety, I thought.

I continued. "Did I say something stupid yesterday? I wonder who I texted at 2 am? Is that deal going to close?" Social anxiety, I thought.

Trevor scrunched his face in disapproval.

"Those are stupid stories, John. Stop telling yourself those stories," he said.

∞

We moved from my office, my mancave, to sit under the large Ficus tree in my backyard that I call the *Zodhi* tree.

As we walked, a matrix of Anxiety and Depression based on the structure of the Metaphysics of Quality appeared in my head.

	Depression	Anxiety
Intellectual	Things can never change	People shouldn't think that
Social	I am a loser	Did I do something stupid?
Organic	I am fat	I ate too much
Inorganic	The world is doomed.	Climate change keeps me up at night

Anxiety is a desire for something to be different than it is. Depression is a belief that things can never change. Both lead to despair.

~ DESPAIR ~

Society is crumbling
I know you see it too
The war machine is rumbling
Our leaders gone coo-coo.

Lives better over centuries
But optimisms popped
Supreme Court taking liberties
Freedom's progress stopped.

The food we're fed is killing us
To grow the drug machine
Corruption's grip is chilling us
These profits are obscene.

The same machine is teaching us
But truth has split in two
Politics dividing us
Like black and white – Red / Blue

So, what's the point of all of this
Life's Lack of Quality
The stories we've been told
Just push anxiety.

The Church of Reason blinds us
To what is plain to see
The beauty that surrounds us
From sea to shining sea.[6]

---

[6] A poem was inspired by the key themes of a transcript of a conversation that author and modern-day philosopher, Charles Eisenstein had with his eighteen-year-old son.

INTRODUCING THE BOOT SEQUENCE

When we sat down under the tree, Trevor continued his point dismissing my anxieties, "Do you know what a *Boot Sequence* is?" he asked?

"Do you mean like the Apple logo that appears on my phone when I turn it on?" I asked?

"Yes, that logo is part of the device's *boot sequence*. The device turns on, and a small set of code gets loaded from long-term storage into live memory and processed to tell the device who it is supposed to be."

I could see where he was heading. My anxieties are my boot sequence. I wake up and remind myself of all my problems I'm having and what I fear or dread the most.

Trevor was getting animated, "Think about it, John. Everything you have ever done started with a story in your head. Going to college, buying a car, getting a job, getting married. It all started with an idea you, or someone else, put in your head."

Like Speedo quitting his job and joining Ski Patrol, I thought, Trevor implied that perhaps I could put a different set of code - a different story - into my long-term brain storage that would reprogram how I saw and behaved in the world.

"So, every morning," Trevor said with religious zeal, "I say my *boot sequence* out loud:

Today is the best day ever.
I am free to do whatever I want.
I am the master of my universe.
I am the narrator of my own epic story."

I was incredulous, "You actually do this?" I asked.

"Yes, every day," he said.

A flood of thought saturated my mind. In the same way that we all have a philosophy, we all have a boot sequence whether we realize it or not.

THE STORIES WE ARE TOLD TO TELL

I reflected on the Boot Sequences I'd been indoctrinated with. Remember the definition of a Good Life that was handed down to me? Like my brothers before me, one thing we were told was to get into a Good College we had to become a Boy Scout and earn the rank of Eagle Scout.

Among the requirements to be a Boy Scout was to memorize and regularly repeat the Scout Oath:

"On my honor, I will do my best to do my duty to God and my country, to obey the Scout Law, to help other

people at all times, to keep myself physically strong, mentally awake, and morally straight."

~ It's like a boot sequence for a Boy Scout. ~

The Scout Law is similar:

"A scout is trustworthy, loyal, helpful, friendly, courteous, kind, obedient, cheerful, thrifty, brave, clean, and reverent."

~ 40 years later, I still remember all of them by heart ~

Similarly, as school children in the 1970s, every day, we'd recite the Pledge of Allegiance:

I pledge allegiance to The Flag of The United States of America, and to The Republic for which it stands. One nation, under God, with liberty and justice for all.

~ Ritual and repetition bind people together. ~

Boot Sequences that people are told to memorize include a statement of values for the community to believe, including:

- Gratitude
- Respect
- Acceptance
- Forgiveness
- Awareness, and
- Confidence

WRITING YOUR OWN BOOT SEQUENCE

It is empowering to realize that we can intentionally *install* new assumptions about the world in our heads. These repeated intentions go deep into our subconscious mind and affect how we see what is happening around us.

~ This is not a way of thinking that is normally taught. ~

But given how somehow, I projected my entire life in my Harvard Business School essay 33 years ago, I began to wonder if a *boot sequence* might *actually* work.

BOOT SEQUENCES AS BIG VISIONS

After explaining the boot sequence, Trevor told me he had bought the domain name Conscious.ly. We brainstormed a big vision for that domain.

As an apostle of a series of founders, I have always been attracted to Big Visions. Trevor and I sat there discussing some of the ones I loved.

- **Second Life's** - "To connect everyone to an online world that improves the human condition."
- **General Assembly's** - "A global community of individuals empowered to pursue the work they love."

Say what you want about Elon Musk these days, but it's hard not to love:

- **Tesla's -** "To accelerate humanity's transition to sustainable energy."

Trevor and I brainstormed for a while about a big vision for the domain name Conscious.ly and simply changed a few words of Tesla's:

"Conscious.ly's mission is to accelerate humanity's evolution to the next level of consciousness," we laughed. Certainly no one could do that. Right?

Then we turned to something more practical for our company at the time, Assembled Brands: "To reinvent venture financing for the 21st century."

I elaborated. "Because as consumers become more aware of where their products come from and where they go, every single product in every single category needs to be reinvented. The incumbent financial system is not set up to finance so many small companies."

If we were really going to change the world by helping brands grow, I had to take a step back and first change myself. As Confucius said:

*"First, there must be order and harmony within
your own mind. Then this order will spread to
your family, then to the community, and finally
to your entire kingdom. Only then can you have
peace and harmony."*

Later I drafted the rest of my boot sequence:

~ TODAY IS THE BEST DAY EVER ~

Today is the best day ever.
I am free to do whatever I want.
I am the master of my universe and
I am the narrator of my own epic story.

I am accelerating humanity's evolution to the next level
of consciousness.
I am re-inventing venture financing.
I am the steward of a family farm.

I am grateful for the gift of four healthy children
I am grateful for my wife and all that she does for me,
our family, and our home.
I am grateful for an abundance of extraordinary friends.

My favorite line also comes from Trevor's:

I am so happy and grateful that money keeps coming to
me in increasing quantities from multiple sources on a
continuous basis.

At that time, my income came 100% from a single company. At the time of this publication, it comes from over 100 companies.

After realizing that everything I'd written about in my application essay to Harvard Business School came true in order, except writing a book, I concluded my boot sequence with:

I am a writer.

CHAPTER 13

Philosofathergizing

Sunset in southern California is a spiritual experience. The *golden hour* transforms ordinary scenes into extraordinary ones. As I was walking the dogs around the neighborhood one golden afternoon, Luke, my 14-year-old son, sped by on his One Wheel. "I got 100 on my math test!" He held out his hand for a high five. His voice almost was modulated by the doppler effect as he sped by.

"I'm so proud of you, Luke, well done!" I said. As he zoomed away, I thought about how sometimes, when Luke is doing his math homework, he gets agitated when he makes a mistake or can't figure something out. He groans out loud and complains about having so much more math to do - a trait likely passed on to him from my younger self.

"Hey Luke, your grades are always going to be good enough..." he zoomed back toward me, as I continued, "...whether or not you resist any of the activities that you must do to get good grades. Just notice what your mindset is, and your grades are going to be fine."

He looked puzzled, so I sought to simplify, "I am not worried about your grades."

Luke stopped right in front of me. "What are you worried about, Dad?" he asked.

I paused, realizing I'd fallen into a semantic trap. "I am not worried about anything, really. I just wish somebody had told me what I'm about to tell you."

I had Luke's attention and thought this better be good, not knowing exactly what I would say.

The word *Gumption* came to mind. In Motorcycle Maintenance, Pirsig spends a long chapter on this word. He wrote, "I like the word 'gumption'...an old Scottish word...because it describes exactly what happens to someone who connects with Quality. He gets filled with gumption. The Greeks called it *enthousiasmos,* the root of "enthusiasm" which means literally, as Pirsig wrote:

> *"...filled with theos, or God, or [arête] or*
> *Quality...A person filled with gumption doesn't*
> *sit around...stewing about things."*

I put my hand on Luke's shoulder and looked him in the eye. Your *mindset* while you're doing the work, is more important than the outcome."

Luke sped off and said, "Can you remind me of that?" I started to say it again. "Your mindset while you are doing the work…"

"No, Dad," Luke interrupted, firing up his One Wheel. "Saying it once, it's not going to change anything," he said. "Repeating it to me now isn't going to change anything. But after I hear it a bunch of times over a long period of time, I might start to get it."

As he sped away, I smiled and thought, *wow, Luke.* I turned toward the setting sun and laughed out loud. My words chased him in the distance "That's exactly right!" I shouted.

Repeating a story to yourself over a long period of time is what people, organizations, companies, religions, and countries do.

It's what they have always done.

~ SONG OF METAPHYSICS ~

At first, this won't be easy
But very soon, you'll see
We're confused by a description
Of reality!

The map is not the territory
The word is not the thing
The financials aren't the business
A new song now to sing

A song of metaphysics
Subject-object not
Quality and stories Reality upsot

Stories create reality
And that's how we arrange it
We're surrounded by a many dream
And we can learn to change it

You might say that it's impossible
But it's our thing to dream it
We've always dreamed a many dream
And then we have achieved it

Now that you have heard it
It won't be hard to see
When we tell a story
We create reality.

CHANGING WHAT YOU VALUE CHANGES THE SYSTEM

Back to Speedo and his U-Haul, plus Pirsig and his machine.

~ *"If you're not happy, get happy."* ~

Like a motorcycle, life is a system that must be tuned and re-tuned. Today, your life is 100% the way it is.

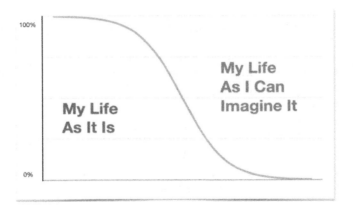

Everything you've ever accomplished started as an intention put in your head by you or someone else.

Your parents influence you initially, then teachers and friends. Eventually, every individual can take the role of narrator in their own epic story.

I certainly wasn't taught this as a young man. I am certainly not claiming any special relationship with these ideas that makes me any better at this than anyone else. It certainly feels like I struggle, confront, and wrestle with the ideas of the world a lot.

I'm just a kid who grew up bounded by a traditional philosophy and view of the world, and then noticed how much my entire life was shaped by a story I wrote to Harvard Business School 33 years ago.

I didn't realize my narrative imagination blossomed then. Yet it was Trevor's boot sequence that brought the reigns of my life from my unconscious to my conscious mind.

I didn't write anything new until I added "I am a writer" to my boot sequence.

~

"I've always thought that each person invented himself... that we are each a figment of our own imagination. And some people have a greater ability to imagine than others."
- David Geffen

~ SUNLIGHT ON MY EYELIDS ~

A poem about the story in your head

Staring at a blank
Imagining a song
It's just me I'm singing to.
How could I go wrong?

There is no one to hear it
This bit inside my head
It's just me I'm singing to
It's nothing 'til it's read.

I hear the music playing
I can see the score
Like sunlight on my eyelids
I'll always want some more.

When anxiety conflicts
And fights my little song
I'll sing a little louder
Please come and sing along.

CHAPTER 14

The Story of Weekly Accounting

It took about four years to cultivate Assembled Brands from concept to initial funding to a team of about a dozen people fully funded with a path to profitability.

Today, Assembled Brands has invested nearly $200 million in over 100 emerging consumer brands.

I'm still on the board, still on the credit committee, and with my team, still act as their CFO. So, now I work there for about one hour per week.

I also left because after looking at the financials of thousands of emerging consumer brands, we realized how poorly accountants and bookkeepers serve small businesses and we saw another huge business opportunity.

~ An opportunity to help a lot more people. ~

A NEW STORY

As I was transitioning from full-time responsibilities at Assembled Brands to one hour per week, Jeff, my nephew, and I began to align the intentions of our partnership.

Jeff started by asking: "How do you want your day to be?"

To which I said, "All The Work would be done for me!"

Yada Yada, "The Work" did we.
It wasn't long, we're in year three.
Now our days and nights are free.
What you speak is what you see
It must be true…it's poetry.

Oops, I didn't mean to spring that poem on you, but when you've got 100 poems explaining your philosophy, it happens. I can feel Luke, and the rest of my family, rolling their eyes at me. "Oh, Dad." Pirsig said,

"When you've got a Chautauqua in your head,
it's extremely hard not to inflict it on innocent
people."

Next, we set a big vision – Weekly Accounting

To help everyone see their business better.

To help people see their business better we developed a better map. A map that uses all the data from the business, not just the bank transactions.

At this point in the story, we are going to introduce a new language and a new map. Consider this a brief overview - almost an introduction to a second book. That second book, *Zen and the Art of Weekly Accounting* is what I had intended to write when I wrapped an empty notebook with a reprint of a painting my daughter made.

If you're less interested in the business aspects, you can skip to the next chapter. That chapter describes our System to Pursue Quality.

A MAP FROM THE TIME OF COLUMBUS

The traditional map of business is called the "Three Statement Model." The three statements that everyone uses to evaluate a business are the income statement, the cash flow statement, and the balance sheet.

This map was first documented by a mathematician in Venice Italy in 1494 - over five hundred years ago! That's right...the map we use for business was invented when most people believed the world was flat.

Balance sheets, like cell phones and ski helmets, must have been adopted slowly. Today, everyone uses them.

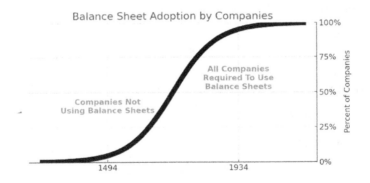

For 500 years all accountants have done is make more rules. Which made me think:

~ A CPA is a license to do your books in a way that doesn't help the business ~

That's because the intention of a CPA is to keep you compliant - to make sure you follow the rules set forth by the tax collectors and government regulatory agencies.

~ A multi-hundred-billion-dollar industry to make sure you follow the rules. ~

I'd rather work in a windowless lab and go home and rake my own leaves than make sure people follow the rules of an arcane system designed 500 years ago.

I am not discounting the value of accountants here. Most care and do great work—important work—and they get a lot right. It's this system of audited financials that has enabled investors to put so much trust - and therefore investment in public companies in the United States.

But though I've been a public company CFO, I was never taught how to think like an accountant. I am an electrical engineer used to working on Sonar Systems - so we started with a different intention.

Our intention was to help you see your business better.

Accountants have been so distracted by making sure you follow the rules that in those 500 years no one thought to double-click on revenue to see something that was common across all businesses in every industry. To cut through the jargon of industries to find a common view of revenue metrics and unit economics.

It's hard enough to explain a balance sheet to someone today. Imagine what it must have been like in 1494. And now imagine you're seeing the fourth statement for the first time. As you read what follows, imagine the specifics in your own business.

THE FOURTH STATEMENT: THE STATEMENT OF ECONOMIC QUALITY

What's great about an income statement, balance sheet and cash flow statement is that it's a common view across all businesses. You know what to expect when you are looking at financial statements - Revenue, COGs, Gross Profit, etc.

Like the first three financial statements, the fourth statement - the Statement of Economic Quality is common across all businesses. It *instruments the Contribution Engine* and has four sections:

- The Audience section,
- The Customer Roll Forward section,
- The Unit Economics section, and
- The Direct Cash section.

The Income Statement answers the questions "Were we profitable or unprofitable over a period of time?" The Balance Sheet answers, "Where are all of our assets and liabilities at this specific point in time?" The Statement of Cash Flows answers, "Where did the cash come from and where did it go?" The Statement of Economic Quality answers,

"Are the underlying economics of the business healthy?"

Now, let's look at each section of the Statement of Economic Quality a little more closely.

- **Audience**: Every company has a potential audience - its addressable market. Each period, we like weekly, the company spends money to get exposed to a portion of its audience.
- **Customer Roll Forward:** Through a marketing funnel and sometimes a sales funnel, a company seeks to convert that audience into new customers and hopefully keep them coming back.
- **Unit Economics:** From those two sections, we can calculate a company's Unit Economics. Unit Economics are a way of looking at a business that focuses on comparing *customer acquisition costs* to the *lifetime gross profit* that customer is expected to generate. We *sample* unit economics over time - weekly, monthly and quarterly - but we also step back and look at Cumulative Unit Economics. Using the cumulative unit economics to compare the value of revenue streams in different industries.
- **Direct Cash Flow Statement:** Finally, we look at cash - through the lens of what Accountants call a Direct Cash Flow Statement. This starts with collections and ends with your change in cash without any accrual adjustments. Like looking at your own checkbook. We do it this way so we can close the books on a company quickly - every week in fact.

A map is "better" when it reflects the underlying nature of the territory it represents. Similarly, drawing from all of a business' data has the potential to create a better map than one created just from the transactions that hit the bank account. The language of the Statement of Economic Quality and the concept of the Contribution Engine is a better representation of a business.

We know it's a better map because it helps people make their businesses better. The reason is a simple 2x2:

~ When you put the right data in front of an empowered team, they get better. ~

You can try it other ways, but it won't work.

	Wrong Data	Right Data
Empowered Team	Frustrating	**Things Get Better**
Not Empowered Team	Fail	Sad

Many times, you can and will try it other ways without even knowing. You'll be looking at the wrong data without knowing that it's wrong. You'll then get frustrated, or you'll unintentionally disempower your team and that's just sad.

But here's the thing - like everything else - it's a process. You start this process of improvement by admitting you have a problem. The map you are using isn't getting you to where you want to go. That's the "Test of the System."

If it's not good, you ask more questions and gather more data to try to make a map that reflects the underlying reality better.

The Fourth Statement, The Statement of Economic Quality illuminates the Contribution Engine of a business. The implications of the contribution engine concept are just as profound today as the balance sheet was 500 years ago. When you use the right map to organize the data, the territory becomes clearer and it gets easier to get from one place to another. Once you see your business this way, you won't be able to unsee it.

Let's look at each part of the organization and how the language of the Contribution Engine can help to align everyone in an organization better.

A NEW ORG CHART

A business is a system with two kinds of people:

People working *in* the Contribution Engine and people working on the Contribution Engine.

People working *in* the Contribution are people who:

- Service customers directly, and
- People who attract and retain customers.

The people working *on* the Contribution Engine are like the Pit Crew that keeps maintains the components of the car as it circles the race track over and over week after week.

People working *on* the Contribution Engine are people who:

- Instrument the Contribution Engine,
- Finance the Contribution Engine,
- Staff the Contribution Engine, and
- Overseeing the system as a whole - like the CEO, board and investors.

By organizing a business around the contribution engine, it is easier to *make the unit of work self-aware* and align the entire organization to achieve the business goals.

We'll have a lot more to say about this in our next book, Zen and the Art of Weekly Accounting.

ECOMMERCE COMPANY CONTRIBUTION ENGINE

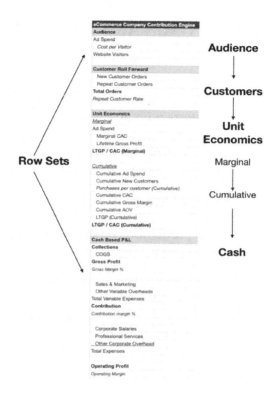

THE WEEKLY ACCOUNTING PERFORMANCE MATRIX

	Troubled	Functional	Integrated	World Class
Data Quality	Traditional Monthly Close done by a CPA	Manual Monday Morning Metrics (MMM)	Automated MMM	"Unit of Work" is "Self Aware"
Feels like	"We won't know revenue until we close the books"	"Where'd you get that data? Is that right?"	"We know where to focus our attention"	"Every role has a set of weekly metrics to manage themselves by"

81

~ THE INTENTION AND THE SYSTEM ~

A poem based on a quotation by Robert Pirsig

It starts with an intention
And turns into The Word
Sample progress in a row set
Precise...like hummingbird.

Compare the row set to intention
An accounting every week
Make predictions of the future
The system then will seek.

If it's not good then you will know
Exactly what to do -
Mind or system has to change, and
The fix is up to you.

CHAPTER 15

A System to Pursue Quality

Robert Pirsig posits that "Metaphysics is good if it improves everyday life; otherwise forget it."

I found that funny because though his books were successful, his metaphysics did not improve the everyday lives of very many people.

Certainly, our understanding of the Metaphysics of Quality, combined with other stories passed to us through generations of storytellers inside and outside our families has improved our everyday lives.

~ But I think Pirsig just planted a seed. ~

What else could he do?

He could see that higher educational institutions in 1974 were teaching from a bad map. So, he wrote, and he wrote. He wrote about his experience, his thought process, years and years of dead ends, and the "gumption" it took to persevere.

In short, he cared. He cared so much he dedicated his life to documenting a completely different way of looking at the world that would have a chance of blossoming to improve everyday life.

When I was reading his books, I wrote in the margins:

"*Pirsig wrote his books for students he would never meet.*"

Pirsig threw an intellectual football deep into the future. With this work, we have caught that football translated for ourselves so we could pass it on again and lay a path for others to follow.

A System to Pursue Quality

Our intention is to build a knowledge transfer system such that the most important work in the Metaphysics of Quality would, in time, appear and keep being generated and re-generated, generation after generation.

That's what we hope [nothing] does.

Books are traditionally static. This is Not-a-Book. Bibles are especially static. This is Not-a-Bible.

In this version of me I'd realize that I am not doing this alone. I am not doing this out of my own ego. I am not doing this for me. I have everything I need, and I have less time to live than I have lived.

I am doing this for my children and my children's children. So that they can live in a world where people create Quality.

It seems in the world today, people create separation and isolation, which, as a result, creates despair. I think it's because of the way we tell the stories we tell and the fundamental beliefs about the world we've been told. These stories we tell passed through generations, create the status quo.

To Increase our Responsibility

Long before we started our partnership, Jeff stated his intention: "To increase our responsibility."

Until just now, I didn't realize what that meant.

We live in a world where we stand in front of those that came before us. We honor our ancestors and the spirit of the land they cultivated and built upon before us to make our lives easier than theirs.

Our responsibility is to learn and pass on ideas and things that will help the future us, and our children and their children, to survive and thrive.

Zen and the Art of [nothing] is a seed crystal for a system that is fundamental to Our Premise.

If the stories we tell create the reality we see

And systems work better than goals

Then build a system to build systems

And practice better storytelling

In addition to describing the Metaphysics of Quality, Pirsig's books also described a system to pursue quality.

We've applied his philosophy and his system to create [nothing] - book zero of an infinite series. Motorcycle Maintenance and Lila are books one and two. Book three, our next book, will explore Weekly Accounting and the New Map for Business.

We also have a bunch of poems in the category of "Fixing Your Relationship with Words" so I expect another flower from that stem.

We put [nothing] in brackets indicating it's a placeholder for your art. The [art] of your life. Sooner or later, you'll realize you are the narrator of your own epic story.

To get started, take an empty notebook and write an intention. Leave room to edit that intention and start writing.

And if you'd like support on your motorcycle trip, join our community at CoAuthor.one.

~ NOT-A-BOOK ~

What you have in your hands is Not-a-Book.
It's Not-a-Book you have to read.
Most of it is blank - you see?
A coaster you may never need.

Put it down for weeks and months, it's fine.
Mine sat blank for about a year,
Hiding away from all my fear,
Until an insight just appeared.

The stories we tell they make us, us
They're ours to write, and this is thus,
A space to fill, a space to chill,
A space for when you have the will.

So, buckle up, release your fear,
It's just a place to rest your beer.
The intention of Not-a-Book, you see,
Is to consider how our lives could be
If we had a new story.

We started writing months ago and
Filled a notebook on the go.
It's pages full so that one's done.
Of course there is another one.

There's room for you to write [your art]
We've left some room for you to start.

APPENDIX
~ OUR ETHOS ~

- We believe the stories we tell create the reality we see
- We believe Big Visions and Positive Unit Economics can change the world
- We believe Systems work better than goals
- We seek Win-Win relationships
- We always bring data to the conversation
- We do it for fun
- We believe in the Spirit of the Gift
- We are so happy and grateful that we are so happy and grateful
- Our pronouns are "We" and "Our" because We are One
- Today is the Best Day Ever.

~ THE GARDENING TIPS ~

- Notice the path you walk each day
- Express delight. Show empathy. Never criticize. It's not the plant's fault. It's your fault.
- Instrument a few critical metrics – start with the pH of your water
- Try things, repeat what works
- Seek expert advice – We should have put this one sooner
- Don't give up because you're not an expert – it's just for fun
- Be discerning with your attention it's easy to try too hard for too long
- Keep planting seeds
- Bigger gardens need more help
- Pruning is the art
- Make the path delightful for yourself
- You are going to get better at it

ACKNOWLEDGEMENTS

I don't think you can *intend* to write a book like this. It seemed to just evolve as soon as I added "I am a writer" to the boot sequence.

We are grateful to Trevor for teaching us the boot sequence. To Brian Swichkow for developing Mythos and teaching us to write in it. To Adam Pritzker for including us in the *100 Year Philosophy* of Assembled Brands.

We are grateful to all the founders of companies we've worked with along the way especially John McIntyre a friend and business partner for 30 years, to Nikesh Parekh and Ian Morris for the first real CFO job and to Philip Rosedale and Ginsu Yoon for the second.

We are grateful to the thought partners who have come along side us as we wrote this story, especially Jake Schwartz, Greg Moser, David Metzler, Ethan Lu, Samantha Dobbs, Anne Taylor and Matt Stamer.

We are grateful to our partners in Weekly Accounting who have navigated a rapidly growing business with us including Phil Zdanowski, Kendra Edelman Smith, Chris Chard, Sam Kaplan and Ari Gordon. We are grateful to all the people who have allowed us to practice the poetry on them. We are thankful to John McKusick for the beautiful cover design. It is the most beautiful part of the book.

And finally, we are grateful to our families for forgiving us for *not actually being the voice* that we sound like in our writing. We do keep getting better at it.

John Zdanowski *Jeff Abrams, June 2024.*

~ TOMORROW LET IT BE ~

I don't think I'll be here long, till 65 or 63
That's less than 8 or 10 years
Of the Best of Me

It could turn out it's longer, we'll just have to see
Either way it's different now, than 25 or 23

I could imagine a few decades, to sail with friends at sea
I'd believe that to console myself from reality

I've got four kids to think about from twenty to ten-three
When the youngest's twenty too - then what am I to He?

For them I would imagine a system beyond me
I'd dedicate my every day to crafting that story

Well sure! Some did this before, it's there to plainly see
Everything passed down to us from our family

The vines with fruits are sweeter for the gardener's care
The water flows, a Good Tree grows to fill the earth
with air

So...

If I have left, a single day, tomorrow let it be
What would I do this time today,
With the Best of Me?

Connect with us at this QR Code

You can *GIFT* this book to someone else there too!

Made in the USA
Middletown, DE
16 July 2024

57349631R00051